The Library of High

Strategies for Recalling Knowledge

Remembering Information for Classroom, Homework, and Test Success

Jared Meyer

The Rosen Publishing Group, Inc.,
New York

This book is dedicated to my father, Jon, for inspiring me to think outside the box to create the star from within.

Published in 2006 by The Rosen Publishing Group, Inc.
29 East 21st Street, New York, NY 10010

First Edition

Library of Congress Cataloging-in-Publication Data

Meyer, Jared.
Strategies for recalling knowledge: remembering information for classroom, homework, and test success / Jared Meyer.
    p. cm. — (The library of higher order thinking skills)
Includes bibliographical references.
ISBN 1-4042-0474-1 (lib. bdg.)
ISBN 1-4042-0657-4 (pbk. bdg.)
1. Memory. 2. Mnemonics.
I. Title. II. Series.
LB1063.M49 2005
370.15'22—dc22

                                                                          2004027379

Manufactured in the United States of America

CONTENTS

INTRODUCTION

If you're at school and your teacher asks you a question, do you prefer that the question be easy or hard? When you're at home or at the library studying for a test, do you hope that the exam that you're preparing for is the easiest or the most difficult one you'll take all year? Many students dislike answering challenging questions, whether it is during a classroom activity or on an exam, because they fear that they may not know the correct answers. Surprisingly, however, students often know the information that applies to a correct answer. What they don't know is how to use that information properly in responding to tough questions.

Recalling knowledge is the act of obtaining information you already know and using it to your advantage. By learning how to recall knowledge and access the information you have already stored in your mind, you'll be able to face challenging questions in school with more confidence. In addition, you'll more likely be able to answer these questions correctly.

This book will introduce you to a series of strategies that can be used in recalling knowledge. You can add the tools you find to your mental toolbox and use them during your next class presentation, homework assignment, or test.

Each strategy that is covered here can be used individually or in a group. Depending on the classroom assignment, homework, or exam that requires you to recall knowledge, some of the strategies may be more appropriate to use than others. The more strategies that you take with you after reading this book, the better off you'll be when facing your next academic challenge.

Recalling Knowledge by Defining, Filling in the Blanks, Identifying, and Labeling

You may already be very familiar with one or two of the strategies mentioned in this chapter, including defining, filling in the blanks, identifying, and labeling. However, if you practice these strategies, you will most likely take a few new tips by applying this information to what you already know.

Defining Information

Have you ever looked up the word "dictionary" in the dictionary? Do you know the definition of the word "definition"? Do you ever use certain words in conversation or in writing assignments but don't know what they mean, like the words "dictionary" and "definition" above? Each year in school, you will either directly or indirectly learn where words or concepts come from

Answer It!

See if you know the words that belong to the following **definitions**.

1) A narrative account of events.
2) Assured reliance on the character, ability, strength, or truth of someone or something.
3) A programmable electronic device that can store, retrieve, and process data.

1. story, 2. trust, 3. computer

and what they mean. By knowing this information, you then will intelligently be able to use such words and concepts in daily conversations, e-mails, and classes.

Defining means giving a detailed description of the meaning of a word or concept. If you open the dictionary, you will find thousands of words and their definitions. The publisher has gone beyond the task of defining the words and included extensive information such as the origins and also the synonyms of the words.

Try It!

Define the following words and see how well you think you know them.

- test
- idea
- person
- life
- history
- love

Even though you think you may know the meanings of these words well, you may have trouble defining them. If you do have trouble, study their definitions. You will then be able to use these words more intelligently.

In school, you may be faced with questions for which you have to define certain concepts. For example, when studying science, a teacher may ask you to define the water cycle or to define the three components needed to start a fire. Defining information correctly can be done by memorizing the information well. Additionally, repetition, or studying the information over and over, will also help you remember definitions. The very same strategy of defining words or concepts can be used when facing challenging questions.

By defining key concepts and terms, you can show your teacher that you understand the topic you are being taught. Try practicing defining words and concepts and see if concepts are more challenging to define than words.

Filling in the Blanks

Have you ever come across a sentence or statement that is missing words, and in place of the words is a blank line such as this ____? On an assignment or in an exam, you may face the challenge of having to find appropriate words to complete a statement by filling in the blanks.

Filling in the blanks is the process of recalling knowledge to find the appropriate words that could be used to make a sentence both

Figure It Out

On a separate sheet of paper, complete the following sentences.

- Earth is the _____ planet from the Sun.
- America has _____ states.
- The opposite of cold is _____ .
- The first president of the United States was _____ .
- Antarctica is in the _____ Hemisphere.

1. third, 2. 50, 3. hot, 4. George Washington, 5. southern

complete and clear. The purpose of filling in the blanks is to challenge you to be creative in recalling the knowledge that can make your sentences, and hence ideas, make sense.

Multiple-choice questions provide all the information required to answer a question. The opposite is true for filling in the blanks. Sometimes the words needed to fill in the blanks are provided. At other times, the correct answers may not be available at all.

For example, a student may come to a question that has more than one answer that could be considered correct. For example, "_____ is a color in a rainbow (red, orange, yellow, green, blue, indigo, or violet)." Each of the colors provided are correct. On the other hand, a question may be very specific, such as "In the year_____, Christopher Columbus discovered America." The only correct answer would be 1492.

The key to remembering the answers to fill-in-the-blank questions is studying the information until you feel like you're an expert on the subject. Using memorization and repeating similar fill-in-the-blank exercises will make it easier for you to recall the information. Then, when you are faced with an exam or a closed-book assignment with similar exercises, you'll be prepared and will remember the answers.

Identifying Information

Imagine that you are bird-watching with a pair of binoculars while using a bird-watching guidebook. The guidebook helps you determine the individual characteristics of the birds and their differences from other birds. By knowing how to identify, or classify, each bird, you can appreciate each one separately. While the guidebook acts as a helpful resource for determining which bird is which, the ability to identify the birds would actually be your greater skill while bird-watching. You wouldn't have to rely on the guidebook.

The same goes for your studies in school. Identifying is the act of recognizing a specific word, phrase, or concept. You can identify information in a variety of ways. You may find a group of items and be asked to identify all of the contents of the group, to categorize only the similar contents of the group, or to pick out one item from the group. In the same way that you would identify the different characteristics of birds while bird-watching, you can identify the different qualities of information while in school and use this skill to recall knowledge.

Another situation in which identifying is used is when you are trying to figure out a word or concept, what it is, and how it relates to the context of the subject. Have you ever heard the expression

Answer It!

Identify which word does not belong in the group.

- running
- walking
- sitting
- jogging
- jumping

Since four of the five words, "running," "walking," "jogging," and "jumping," can be **identified** as physical activities, "sitting" would be **identified** as the one word that does not belong in the group of similar terms.

"thinking outside of the box"? This expression means thinking more creatively than usual. When identifying a word, think outside of the box by asking yourself questions such as "How does one word relate to another word?" and "Am I familiar with this word, and have I seen or used it before?" Having the understanding and knowledge of identifying information allows you successfully to answer questions on exams, assignments, and homework.

Answer It!

- **Identify** the state capital of New York on a map.
- **Identify** which of the following objects is yellow: apple, orange, watermelon, banana, and peach.
- On a map of the United States, **identify** which states border an ocean or gulf.

Labeling Information

Labeling is similar to identifying. With labeling, though, you categorize information with a very specific term or title. By labeling, you can maintain consistency in being able to recognize information easily over and over again.

Labeling may be helpful if you have a reading assignment in which a question might be something like, "Label the names of the characters below their photographs." You would then attempt to label each photo with the appropriate name of the character by using the characteristics that were included in the reading.

Also similar to identifying, labeling can be used to determine the differences and similarities between items on a list. If you have a list including the terms "cat," "dog," "cookie," "brownie," and "bird," you could be asked to separate the items by

Try It!

Try these practice examples related to **labeling**:

- Thinking of all your friends, **label** which ones are female and which ones are male.
- On a blank sheet of paper, **label** the days of the week in chronological order. Then, right below the days, write a number indicating your favorite day to your least favorite. Your most favorite would be number one.
- Write down all your classes and **label** them with numbers from most favorite to least favorite.
- Which would you **label** as a better writing utensil: a pen or a pencil?

general similarities. You could label "cat," "dog," and "bird" as animals or pets. "Cookie" and "brownie" could be labeled as desserts or food.

The strategy of labeling can also be used to break down a reading assignment into several parts. While reading a document, you could jot down short notes or labels about general information that you are absorbing as you read along. The labels could be reviewed later on as reminders of what you read in each paragraph.

Recalling Knowledge by Listing, Locating, Matching, and Memorizing

By now you have been introduced to four of the thirteen strategies for recalling knowledge, and you may have just realized that you had already been using them every day at school before ever learning that they were actually strategies. You may find that more of the strategies are normal day-to-day terms that you are familiar with, while others may be new to you. Consider them all valuable tools, especially the next four that will be covered: listing, locating, matching, and memorizing.

Listing Information

Have you ever made a list of things to do? How about a list of people's birthdays? Listing is compiling a group of items and is done to help you organize and remember information. A list can act as an answer to a question on an assignment. Therefore, lists have come to be known as excellent tools for recalling knowledge, especially when it comes to schoolwork.

Listing is very easy to do and can play an important role in answering challenging questions, completing difficult assignments, or even when studying information for an exam. We are often able to study quickly if we have items clearly presented to us in some sort of organized fashion. Listing can play the perfect role as a study guide by noting significant terms of the material you are studying. For example, while studying the variety of systems in the human body, you could make a list of some of them on a sheet of paper as you read about each of them in your textbook, such as:

- Respiratory system

- Cardiovascular system

- Muscular system

- Reproductive system

- Nervous system

- Digestive system

- Excretory system

- Endocrine system

Lists that are created in columns, like the one on page 16, are the easiest to use when studying, and will help you remember information. You may have tests that ask you to list information such as the states that seceded from the Union during the Civil War, the planets in order starting with the closest one to the Sun, or the verbs in a paragraph like the one you are reading now.

Locating Information

Another strategy that is used to recall information is called locating. Locating is something you probably do every day. When you are looking for your sneakers or the key to your home, you are trying to locate it. That is, you are attempting to successfully find your possessions.

Write It!

- Make a **list** your favorite movies. Next, out of those you've **listed**, make another **list** of those movies that you have seen more than three times.
- Think of your favorite movie. **List** the movie's most important scenes.
- How many of your classmates can you **list** without looking around your classroom?
- Make a **list** of the things you would like to do today.
- **List** all of the characters in the last book you read.

Locating is the act of searching for and finding something that you want or need. This skill can be very helpful in preparing for exams, homework assignments, and classroom projects because it is a basic strategy that can be applied to finding the right information when trying to answer a question or solve a problem.

You've probably already mastered the act of locating reference books for a research project or locating a continent such as Africa on a globe. You may have easier test questions that ask you to locate information on maps, though locating specific information in a two- or three-page story is often more challenging. You may have an exam in which you are required to read a long passage and answer questions. Some of the questions may ask you to refer directly to the information that you have just read. Therefore, you will have to return to the passage and locate the information you need to answer the question.

Other questions, like those that have multiple choices available, may have answers that appear similar to the information in the passage. Sometimes, however, the correct choice is the one with identical information to that in the reading. Unless you have a great memory, you may have to revisit the passage and locate the correct information.

Another question that could be asked to test your knowledge of the passage is something such as,

Try It!

- Find a map of the United States and **locate** the states Florida, California, and Texas.
- Take out a magazine, open it, and find and read an article that you find interesting. When you are finished, **locate** the characters that were mentioned in the article by circling their names with a pencil.
- What is the fastest way to **locate** your parent or guardian?
- How would you suggest to a new classmate how to **locate** the school cafeteria?

"Who in the passage said he was unhappy about the rainy weather?" If you don't remember everything you read, you would return to the source and try to locate who said that exact statement. If you're asked a question that is not so specific, attempt to locate the answer in the reading by looking for similarities to the question.

Students can locate information by returning to the source, reviewing the material that is being used, and scanning each line for words and phrases that are related to the exercise.

Matching Information

Are the socks you are wearing right now the same color? Do you ever accidentally wear two different colored socks because you didn't take the time to match them up? Matching is the act of comparing two things, either objects or information, to determine whether they have any similarities.

You probably see examples of matching at home. Do you ever notice how your pillowcases often match your bedsheets or your soup bowls match your dinner plates? While matching can be done to help objects in your home look like they belong in the right place, it can also be

Write It!

Make two lists, one being a list of colors and the second being a separate list of types of clothing. Based on what you are wearing right now, using a pencil, draw a line from the name of a piece of clothing that you are currently wearing that is on one list to the appropriate color that is on the other list. By the end of this exercise, for example, if you were wearing green shorts, the word "shorts" and the word "green" would be connected by a single line.

used to recall information and answer questions correctly on school assignments.

Not only can matching be used to figure out if two or more things have anything in common, it can also be applied to see if items have more differences than similarities. On a homework assignment, you may be asked to break down a group of information into additional groups based on the characteristics they have in common. For example, you could be given two lists. One list could be of cities in the world and the other a list of countries. Your task would be to match the cities to the countries they're in. You

Try It!
....

Take a deck of playing cards and place them all faceup on the floor or on a table. Attempt to **match** all the kings with other kings; try to **match** all the 2s with the other 2s, and so on. By the end of the exercise you should have thirteen piles of cards, each with four different suits, or markings, but with similar numbers (a pile of 2s, 3s, 4s, 5s, 6s, 7s, 8s, 9s, 10s, jacks, queens, kings, and aces).

would see that New York City would be matched with the United States, London would be matched with England, and Buenos Aires would be matched with Argentina.

Matching can be used to categorize information and is often found on examinations. If you are required to give an oral presentation and you want to explain the similarities or differences between two or more things, a good visual exercise would be to present a task similar to the one noted above about geography on a chalkboard. Making a connection between the items on each list by drawing a line would clarify their relationship and assist in recalling that information for future usage.

Memorizing Information

Do you remember how old you were when you learned how to tie your shoelaces? Do you know how you were able to train yourself, or memorize, how to do it? Memorizing is the act of studying information to be able to recall it at any time, and it is a very important strategy you can use in schoolwork.

Compared to the other strategies that have been covered in this book so far, memorizing is one that will rarely be included directly on an exam. This is because memorizing is a strategy that you would use before taking the test, thereby allowing you to already be prepared to answer questions.

Throughout each day, we all have things to remember, such as not to forget our keys or to do our homework. So what we do is try to remember these things in order to complete these tasks when we need to. When it comes to schoolwork, memorizing can be used in many different ways. It can be used for answering questions correctly on tests, giving good presentations, and completing homework assignments without having to rely on other reference materials.

Try It!

- Look at a map of the state that you live in and spend five minutes **memorizing** as many cities as you can. Now try the exercise again for an additional five minutes. Were you able to **memorize** even more cities than before?

- Do you know all the birthdays of your family members? If not, find out what they are and **memorize** them. Then take out a calendar and see if you can remember them all. Memorize them by putting more time into repeating them by actively writing them down and saying them aloud.

Memorizing certain information can be easy for some students and difficult for others. This depends on the amount and type of the information you are trying to remember. In other words, how hard memorizing information is depends on how much there is to memorize and how in-depth the information is. You may find some information easier to remember than other information.

Here are a few examples of questions that could appear on a homework assignment or exam that would require you to have memorized the appropriate information.

• In what year was America founded as an independent nation?

• Who was the first president of the United States?

• What is Betsy Ross known for accomplishing?

The answers to the questions noted above would be easy as long as you spent time studying and successfully memorizing the information before being asked the questions. It's been said that one of the easiest ways to memorize information is by repeating the information over and over, both by writing it down and by saying it. This is known as repetition. Repetition and memorization go hand in hand.

To remember the answer to the first question on the preceding page, you could write down "1776," the correct answer, on a sheet of paper twenty times. You could also do this for the answers to the second and third questions: "George Washington" for the second and "fashioning the first American flag" for the third. While writing it down each time, say the word(s) aloud as well. By the time you are finished with such an exercise, you will probably have memorized the information successfully. If not, try the exercise again, and write it out an additional ten times. You will notice that the more effort you put into memorizing information, the quicker you will remember it.

Chapter 3

Recalling Knowledge by Naming and Spelling

Are you noticing any connections between the strategies covered thus far in the book? You may find that some strategies are better when used alone while others would be most helpful when used with a combination of strategies. As you continue learning about the strategies for recalling knowledge, you may be able to come up with your own style of using them in your schoolwork. The next two strategies are sure to be helpful whether you use them one at a time or together.

Naming Information

Another common strategy that can be related to labeling and identifying is naming. Naming is done to specifically identify something. When you want to identify something or give it a title, consider naming it with a single word that would be most appropriate.

Coincidentally, when asked to name something or a group of things, the end result may be the formation of a list—you may remember that listing, a strategy of recalling knowledge,

Write It!

On a separate sheet of paper, **name** all the male members of your family. After you're done with that, **name** all the female members.

was already covered in the beginning of this book. For example, if you are asked to write an essay about a book you have finished reading, you may want to write a brief paragraph about the main characters before elaborating on the importance of their roles in the story. Therefore, you would name each character and could very well list them. Here is an example: "There were three main characters in the story. The young girl, Katie; her mother, Susan; and her father, Jon, were the three most important people mentioned in the book."

Answer It!

- **Name** the last three people you spoke to today.
- **Name** the biggest planet in our solar system.
- **Name** your favorite teacher this year.

Naming is most often a very basic task. In the classroom, for example, you could have a debate about which of the first three presidents of the United States was the most effective leader. To present your ideas and opinions clearly, you would first name the three presidents and only then proceed with explaining your thoughts and supporting arguments. Naming aloud is an excellent method for memorizing information and recalling knowledge.

Spelling Out Words

Does your school have a spelling bee competition? Have you ever competed in such an event? One of the most often-used strategies for recalling information is spelling. Each day, when we communicate to others by writing, we try to make sure that the words we use are not only appropriate in getting our meaning across, but that they are spelled correctly, too.

Did you know that the English language is challenging to learn not only because we can express one thought in many ways, but also because our vocabulary is so vast? One of the reasons our vocabulary is enormous is due to the variety of words we use. Some words are pronounced the same but have different meanings and are sometimes spelled differently. These are called homonyms. Knowing that homonyms exist, and knowing which word means what, allows you to use such words appropriately when you are writing a letter, taking a written exam, or writing an example on the chalkboard in class.

As we identify words or attempt to memorize words correctly, part of having a good vocabulary is knowing how to spell words so they make sense in the context in which you use them. You have probably seen word scramble games or puzzles in which there is a group of letters that don't make sense. The purpose of the game is to place the letters in an appropriate order. By doing this properly, you prove that you not only figured out the word, but also that you know how to spell it correctly.

Games like this can actually help in remembering how to spell words correctly. An example could be "What is this item on which meals are

Try It!

First, without memorizing the correct **spelling** of the word, have a friend or family member ask you to **spell**, "entrepreneur." If they test you three times and you **spell** the word right each time, congratulations! If you don't **spell** it right, use the tips mentioned in this section to learn the proper **spelling** of the word and have someone test you again.

eaten?" B-A-L-T-E. If you were to switch the letters around, you could possibly come up with a word that is made up of the letters b, a, l, t, and e. The answer is "table."

When learning how to spell words correctly, you may notice that the longer the word is, the more difficult it usually is to remember how to spell it. One key to spelling words correctly is breaking down the words into parts when trying to remember them. For example, take the word "encyclopedia." "Encyclopedia" can be tough to remember. While attempting to memorize this word, see if it's easier to memorize the spelling of the word by breaking it down into its syllables like this: en-cy-clo-pe-di-a. Saying each syllable aloud while trying to remember it could make it even easier to spell.

Another way to learn the spelling of words is to use a tip mentioned earlier in the memorization section of this book: repetition. Repetitiously writing and rewriting a word will allow you to learn the word as long as you repeat it correctly.

Spelling is such an important facet of education that you may have spelling exams even in high school. Spelling and vocabulary go hand in hand, and as long as you communicate, they will always be very important, not only in how you use the English language, but also how you remember and recall information.

Recalling Knowledge by Stating, Telling, and Underlining

By combining the previous ten strategies that you have just learned as well as the final three strategies that are covered in this chapter, you will have all the necessary strategies for recalling knowledge. Imagine what you can do in school when you master all thirteen strategies covered in this book, including the final three: stating, telling, and underlining. While you may know a little about them already, you will be able to apply them to your studies for even better results when you finish this book.

Stating Information

Have you ever seen a court television drama in which court is in session and someone asks the person on the witness stand, "State your name and occupation for the record"? Stating is often the act of expressing information directly and concisely. At other times,

Write It!

Answer the questions at the end of the following story:

Andrew aced every one of his exams; John was not such a great test taker. Andrew and John sat next to each other in class and had a math exam coming up the next day. Andrew was so confident that he would do well that he didn't even study. John, on the other hand, studied for hours every night, but he was still not sure he knew the material.

When the teacher handed out the test, Andrew answered the questions quickly. John took much longer, but erased his answers and copied off of Andrew's exam.

When Andrew and John were handed their tests back, they had both failed. When the teacher wrote the correct answers on the board, John realized that his original answers had been correct.

- State what the characters are like in the story.
- State the lesson of the story.
- State the series of events that take place in the story.

when one is asked to state information, greater details may be included to help support the original information.

Stating is a strategy that is similar to naming and identifying. It is unique because by stating, you are given greater options than naming and identifying in expressing yourself. Whereas naming is used to explain a brief term or idea, stating can be used to communicate a term or concept in greater detail than the other two strategies. Further, stating is a great way to learn and remember information.

Stating can be done both verbally and in written form. In many academic activities, it's required to introduce the purpose of the activity or to summarize one's contributions to it. For example, imagine that you're required to work on a group project with a few other classmates. If the project is to be presented to the class when it is due, one of your responsibilities may be to state the purpose of your specific project, to state the responsibilities of each team member, or to state why you chose the topic.

Stating information on exams is very popular as well. After reading a story, for example, you may be asked to do tasks such as making a timeline of the events in a story or stating who the hero in a story is. By stating information correctly, you are expressing to your teacher that you understand the information you have read and that you are able to communicate clearly what you have learned.

Try It!

Here are a couple of practice examples related to **stating**.

• **State** the theme of a book that you are currently reading in one of your classes.
• **State** your teacher's reaction to your last assignment. Was your teacher pleased with your work? Why?
• **State** the names of the countries in North America.

Telling Information

Another strategy in learning how to recall knowledge is telling. "Telling" is another term for "expressing information to someone." When was the last time someone told you a story? Do you enjoy telling your friends secrets?

Telling is the act of giving descriptions that tend to be more lengthy than stating or especially naming information. Telling is often required in homework assignments, classroom projects, and on exams in order to prove that you know information about the topic being covered. On a homework assignment that has a chart of information, you may be asked to tell why the information in the chart is categorized in the manner in which it is presented to you. In the classroom, after a student gives a presentation, your teacher may ask the class, "Tell me the importance of Jenny's project and how it's related to the information that we're learning in class this week." Or, on an exam, you may be asked not only to state certain facts, but also to tell, or explain, why those facts are important.

Try It!

- **Tell** a friend why you feel it's important that he or she not share your secrets with other people.
- **Tell** your family what happened after school today.
- **Tell** your parents what career you want to pursue in the future and why.

Underlining Information

Underlining can be used to prioritize. Prioritizing is focusing on what's most important. Prioritizing can be used to help us memorize information. It can also be used to speed up your review of information.

Underlining is done not only to help you study and remember information in the present, but also to save time in the future when you return to the reading. Underlining is another form of highlighting information, but without using a marker or fluorescent highlighter. It is often done to focus on

Write It!

Write a paragraph briefly describing where you went and what you did on your last vacation, and **underline** the key words and phrases.

the most important data presented to you in a reading or group of information.

If you're studying and you come across the passage, "The beach is a beautiful place. There are many people there who have fun, and it's a great place to visit during the summer," you could underline the key elements. Phrases you would underline are those such as: "beautiful place," "many people," and "visit during the summer." Here's what it would look like: "The beach is a <u>beautiful place</u> to visit. There are <u>many people</u> there who have fun, and it's a great place to <u>visit during the summer</u>." Often used to save time and a lot of unnecessary extra effort, the act of underlining is done to remember information or, at the very least, to quickly recall where the information is located.

Conclusion

Here are the thirteen strategies that were covered in the book: define, fill in the blank, identify, label, list, locate, match, memorize, name, spell, state, tell, and underline. Some of them may be strategies you already use on a daily basis. Others may take a little discipline to include in your schoolwork. And a few may take a little practice to get the hang of. As you have learned, the more actively you try to remember information, the easier it will be for you to recall the knowledge that you have worked so hard to store in your mind.

We all have both short- and long-term memories, and the more effort you put into mastering the information that is covered in your classes, the easier it will be to maintain a long-term memory of what you study. The key tasks to mastering and remembering the material you are faced with in class, at home, or on exams is accessing the information you study. You can do this by manipulating the information so that you can recall it and express it intelligently. By using these strategies, you will gain the confidence of knowing that you have mastered what you have studied. When the time comes for you to prove what you know, you will easily be able to recall the knowledge and apply it to the assignments, presentations, and exams that you will face in school throughout your entire education.

Learning is a lifelong process. After graduating from school, you will also be able to use these strategies as an adult. When you begin your career, you will have a job that will involve mastering specific skills and tasks. Those skills, both simple and complicated, will involve recalling knowledge. As a leader and team member, recalling knowledge such as people's names and birthdays are just a few of the pieces of information you will learn and be able to recall while working with others. If you are responsible for working with numbers, you would recall the knowledge of how to process certain calculations. By using the strategies covered in this book now in school, you will have the tools to learn and recall knowledge throughout your entire life.

GLOSSARY

advantage A benefit, gain, or lead.

chronological Arranged in the order of time.

coincidentally Occurring at the same time.

confidence Self-assurance or self-belief.

discipline Obedience, constraint, or control.

entrepreneur A person who creates business.

extensive Widespread or far-reaching.

facet An aspect, feature, or component of something.

fluorescent Bright, glowing, or luminous.

homonym A word that has the same pronunciation as another word and which may be spelled the same or differently.

occupation Job, profession, or livelihood.

recognize To distinguish, identify, or be aware of.

repetitiously Repeatedly or continually.

strategy A careful plan or method.

syllable A natural beat that is contained in words.

synonym A word that has the same or a very similar definition as another word.

verb A word that describes an action.

WEB SITES

Due to the changing nature of Internet links, the Rosen Publishing Group, Inc., has developed an online list of Web sites related to the subject of this book. This site is updated regularly. Please use this link to access the list:

http://www.rosenlinks.com/lhots/strk

FOR FURTHER READING

Buzan, Tony. *Use Your Perfect Memory*. New York, NY: Plume, 1991.

Davis, Leslie, et al. *Study Strategies Made Easy* (School Success Series). North Branch, MN: Specialty Press, 1996.

Ernst, John. *Middle School Study Skills*. Westminster, CA: Teacher Created Resources, 1996.

Fisher, Alec. *Critical Thinking: An Introduction*. New York, NY: Cambridge University Press, 2001.

Forte, Imogene, Anna Quinn, and Sandra Schurr. *180 Icebreakers to Strengthen Critical Thinking and Problem-Solving Skills*. Nashville, TN: Incentive Publications, Inc., 1999.

Gilbert, Sara. *How to Do Your Best on Tests*. New York, NY: HarperTrophy, 1998.

James, Elizabeth, and Carol Barkin. *How to Be School Smart*. New York, NY: HarperTrophy, 1998.

Lorayne, Harry. *Super-Memory—Super Student: How to Raise Your Grades in 30 Days*, Vol. 1. New York, NY: Little, Brown & Company, 1990.

Luckie, William, et al. *Study Power: Study Skills to Improve Your Learning and Your Grades.* Newton Upper Falls, MA: Brookline Books, 1997.

BIBLIOGRAPHY

Field, John, and Mal Leicester. *Lifelong Learning: Education Across the Lifespan*. London, England: Falmer Press, 2000.

Focus on the Family's Focus on Your Child. "The Secret to Your Child's Academic Success." Retrieved February 9, 2005 (http://www.focusonyourchild.com/learning/art1/A0000420.html).

HOTS: Higher Order Thinking Skills. Retrieved December 6, 2004 (http://www.hots.org).

Pam Petty's Web Page. "Welcome to Higher Order Thinking Skills." Retrieved December 6, 2004 (http://www.pampetty.com/hots.htm).

Southeastern Louisiana University. "What Is Higher Order Thinking?" Retrieved December 6, 2004 (http://www.selu.edu/Academics/Education/TEC/think.htm).

The Informal Education Homepage. "Lifelong Learning @ The Informal Education Homepage." Retrieved February 9, 2005 (http://www.infed.org/lifelonglearning/b-life.htm).

Welcome to Memphis City Schools. "Higher Order
    Thinking Skills." Retrieved December 6, 2004
    (http://www.memphis-schools.k12.tn.us/schools/
    magnolia.es/highorder.htm).

INDEX

About the Author

Jared Meyer is an author and educator who works with students on improving their decision-making and communication skills. As a program facilitator, he has lectured at University of California, San Diego and University of Maryland, College Park. In addition to writing *Strategies for Recalling Knowledge* and *Strategies for Synthesis*, Jared also wrote the book *University of Maryland: Off the Record*. While attending the university, he also had thirteen articles published on student development.

Designer: Nelson Sá; Editor: Nicholas Croce